Alfred Caldecott, Randolph Caldecott, James Davis Cooper

Some of Aesop's Fables

With Modern Instances Shewn in Designs by Randolph Caldecott

Alfred Caldecott, Randolph Caldecott, James Davis Cooper

Some of Aesop's Fables
With Modern Instances Shewn in Designs by Randolph Caldecott

ISBN/EAN: 9783744794633

Printed in Europe, USA, Canada, Australia, Japan

Cover: Foto ©Thomas Meinert / pixelio.de

More available books at **www.hansebooks.com**

SOME OF

ÆSOP'S FABLES

WITH

MODERN INSTANCES

SHEWN IN DESIGNS

BY

RANDOLPH CALDECOTT

FROM NEW TRANSLATIONS BY ALFRED CALDECOTT, M.A.

THE ENGRAVINGS BY J. D. COOPER

London

MACMILLAN AND CO.

1883

INDEX.

NOTE.

SIXTEEN of these Twenty Fables have been handed down to us in a Greek form: for these Halm's text has been used. As to the other four—Number IX. is from Phaedrus, and retains a flavour of artificiality; Numbers XIII. and XX. are from Latin versions; and Number X. is from a French one.

The Translations aim at replacing the florid style of our older English versions, and the stilted harshness of more modern ones, by a plainness and terseness more nearly like the character of the originals.

In the following cases the Translations have been adapted to the Designs. In Number I. *cheese* has been put for *meat;* in Number VIII. a *pack of Hounds* for a *Lion;* in Number XI. a *Stork* for a *Crane;* in Number XIX. a *Frog* for a *Toad;* and in Number VII. the Dog should be *tied up.* The reason of this is, that in the collaboration the Designer and Translator have not been on terms of equal authority; the former has stood unshakeably by English tradition, and has had his own way.

A. C.

THE FOX AND THE CROW

Queen of the Birds, and doubtless it would have been done if she had only had a voice.   The Crow, anxious to prove to him that she did possess a voice, began to caw vigorously, of course dropping the cheese.   The Fox pounced upon it and carried it off, remarking as he went away, " My good friend Crow, you have every good quality : now try to get some common sense."

THE ASS IN THE LION'S SKIN

THE ASS IN THE LION'S SKIN.

AN Ass who had dressed himself up in a Lion's skin was mistaken by everybody for a lion, and there was a stampede of both herds and men. But presently the skin was whisked off by a gust of wind, and the Ass stood exposed; and then the men all charged at him, and with sticks and cudgels gave him a sound drubbing.

THE FISHERMAN AND THE LITTLE FISH

THE FISHERMAN AND THE LITTLE FISH.

A FISHERMAN cast his net and caught a little Fish. The little Fish begged him to let him go for the present, as he was so small, and to catch him again to more purpose later on, when he was bulkier. But the Fisherman said: "Nay, I should be a very simpleton to let go a good thing I have got and run after a doubtful expectation."

THE JACKDAW AND THE DOVES.

THE JACKDAW AND THE DOVES.

A JACKDAW observing how well cared for were the Doves in a certain dovecote, whitewashed himself and went to take a part in the same way of living. The Doves were friendly enough so long as he kept silence, taking him for one of themselves; but when he once forgot himself and gave a croak they immediately perceived his character, and cuffed him out. So the Jackdaw, having failed in getting a share of good things there, returned to his brother

Jackdaws. But these latter not recognising him, because of his colour, kept him out of their mess also; so that in his desire for two things he got neither.

THE COPPERSMITH AND HIS PUPPY

D

THE COPPERSMITH AND HIS PUPPY.

A CERTAIN Coppersmith had a Puppy. While the Coppersmith was at work the Puppy lay asleep; but when meal-
time came he woke up. So his master, throwing him a bone, said :
" You sleepy little wretch of a Puppy, what shall I do with you,
you inveterate sluggard ? When I am thumping on my anvil you
can go to sleep on the mat; but when I come to work my teeth
immediately you are wide awake and wagging your tail at me."

THE FROGS DESIRING A KING

THE FROGS DESIRING A KING.

THE Frogs were grieved at their own lawless condition, so they
sent a deputation to Zeus begging him to provide them with
a King. Zeus, perceiving their simplicity, dropped a Log of wood
into the pool. At first the Frogs were terrified by the splash, and
dived to the bottom; but after a while, seeing the Log remain
motionless, they came up again, and got to despise it so much
that they climbed up and sat on it. Dissatisfied with a King like

that, they came again to Zeus and entreated him to change their ruler for them, the first being altogether too torpid. Then Zeus was exasperated with them, and sent them a Stork, by whom they were seized and eaten up.

THE DOG AND THE WOLF

THE DOG AND THE WOLF.

A WOLF, seeing a large Dog with a collar on, asked him: "Who put that collar round your neck, and fed you to be so sleek?" "My master," answered the Dog. "Then," said the Wolf, "may no friend of mine be treated like this; a collar is as grievous as starvation."

THE STAG LOOKING INTO THE WATER

THE STAG LOOKING INTO THE WATER.

A STAG parched with thirst came to a spring of water. As he was drinking he saw his own reflection on the water, and was in raptures with his horns when he observed their splendid size and shape, but was troubled about his legs, they seemed so thin and weak. As he was still musing, some huntsmen with a pack of hounds appeared and disturbed him, whereupon the Stag took to flight, and keeping a good distance ahead so long as the plain was free from trees, he was being saved; but when he came to a woody place he got his horns entangled in the branches, and being unable to move was seized by the hounds. When he was at the point of death he said to himself: "What a fool am I, who was on the way to be saved by the very things which I thought would fail me; while by those in which I so much trusted I am brought to ruin."

THE FROGS AND THE FIGHTING BULLS

F

THE FROGS AND THE FIGHTING BULLS.

A FROG in his marsh looking at some Bulls fighting, exclaimed: " O dear! what sad destruction threatens us now!" Another Frog asked him why he said that, seeing that the Bulls were only fighting for the first place in the herd, and that they lived quite remote from the Frogs. "Ah," said the first, "it is true that our positions are wide apart, and we are different kinds of things, but still, the Bull who will be driven from the rule of the pasture will come to lie in hiding in the marsh, and crush us to death under his hard hoofs, so that their raging really does closely concern the lives of you and me."

THE LION AND OTHER BEASTS

THE LION AND OTHER BEASTS.

THE Lion one day went out hunting along with three other
Beasts, and they caught a Stag. With the consent of the
others the Lion divided it, and he cut it into four equal portions;
but when the others were going to take hold of their shares,
"Gently, my friends," said the Lion; "the first of these portions
is mine, as one of the party; the second also is mine, because of
my rank among beasts; the third you will yield me as a tribute

to my courage and nobleness of character; while, as to the fourth,—
why, if any one wishes to dispute with me for it, let him begin,
and we shall soon see whose it will be.

THE FOX AND THE STORK

THE FOX AND THE STORK.

THE Fox poured out some rich soup upon a flat dish, tantalising the Stork, and making him look ridiculous, for the soup, being a liquid, foiled all the efforts of his slender beak. In return for this, when the Stork invited the Fox, he brought the dinner on the table in a jug with a long narrow neck, so that while he himself easily inserted his beak and took his fill, the Fox was unable to do the same, and so was properly paid off.

"With Mr Fox's respects & many happy returns of the day"

"With Mrs Stork's kind regards and the compliments of his station"

THE HORSE AND THE STAG

THE HORSE AND THE STAG.

THERE was a Horse who had a meadow all to himself until a Stag came and began to injure the pasture. The Horse, eager to punish the Stag, asked a man whether there was any way of combining to do this. "Certainly," said the Man, "if you don't object to a bridle and to my mounting you with javelins in my hand." The Horse agreed, and was mounted by the Man; but, instead of being revenged on the Stag, he himself became a servant to the Man.

THE COCK AND THE JEWEL

THE COCK AND THE JEWEL.

A BARN-DOOR Cock while scratching up his dunghill came upon a Jewel. "Oh, why," said he, "should I find this glistening thing? If some jeweller had found it he would have been beside himself with joy at the thought of its value: but to me it is of no manner of use, nor do I care one jot about it; why, I would rather have one grain of barley than all the jewels in the world."

THE ASS, THE LION, AND THE COCK

THE ASS, THE LION, AND THE COCK.

AN Ass and a Cock were in a shed. A hungry Lion caught sight of the Ass, and was on the point of entering the shed to devour him. But he took fright at the sound of the Cock crowing (for people say that Lions are afraid at the voice of a Cock), and turned away and ran. The Ass, roused to a lofty contempt of him for being afraid of a Cock, went out to pursue him; but when they were some distance away the Lion ate him up.

THE WOLF AND THE LAMB

THE WOLF AND THE LAMB.

A WOLF seeing a Lamb drinking at a brook, took it into his head that he would find some plausible excuse for eating him. So he drew near, and, standing higher up the stream, began to accuse him of disturbing the water and preventing him from drinking.

The Lamb replied that he was only touching the water with the tips of his lips ; and that, besides, seeing that he was standing

down stream, he could not possibly be disturbing the water higher
up.   So the Wolf, having done no good by that accusation, said:
"Well, but last year you insulted my Father."   The Lamb replying
that at that time he was not born, the Wolf wound up by saying:
"However ready you may be with your answers, I shall none the
less make a meal of you."

THE MAN AND HIS TWO WIVES

THE MAN AND HIS TWO WIVES.

A MAN whose hair was turning gray had two Wives, one young and the other old. The elderly woman felt ashamed at being married to a man younger than herself, and made it a practice whenever he was with her to pick out all his black hairs; while the younger, anxious to conceal the fact that she had an elderly husband, used, similarly, to pull out the gray ones. So, between them, it ended in the Man being completely plucked, and becoming bald.

THE FOX WITHOUT A TAIL

THE FOX WITHOUT A TAIL.

A FOX had had his tail docked off in a trap, and in his disgrace began to think his life not worth living. It therefore occurred to him that the best thing he could do was to bring the other Foxes into the same condition, and so conceal his own deficiency in the general distress. Having assembled them all together he recommended them to cut off their tails, declaring that a tail was an ungraceful thing; and, further, was a heavy appendage, and quite superfluous. To this one of them rejoined: "My good friend, if this had not been to your own advantage you would never have advised us to do it."

"Nonsense. my dears! Husbands are ridiculous things & are quite unnecessary!"

THE EAGLE AND THE FOX

THE EAGLE AND THE FOX.

A N Eagle and a Fox entered into a covenant of mutual affection and resolved to live near one another, looking upon close intercourse as a way of strengthening friendship. Accordingly the former flew to the top of a high tree and built her nest, while the latter went into a bush at the foot and placed her litter there.

One day, however, when the Fox was away foraging, the Eagle, being hard pressed for food, swooped down into the bush, snatched up the cubs and helped her own fledglings to devour them. When the Fox came back and saw what had happened she was not so much vexed at the death of her young ones as at the impossibility of requital. For the Eagle having wings and she none, pursuit was impossible. So she stood some distance away and did all that is left for the weak and impotent to do—poured curses on her foe. But the Eagle was not to put off for long the punishment due to her violation of the sacred tie of friendship. It happened that some country-people were sacrificing a goat, and the Eagle flew down and carried away from the altar some of the burning flesh. But when she had got it to her eyrie a strong wind got up and kindled into flame the thin dry twigs of the nest, so that the eaglets, being too young to be able to fly, were roasted, and fell to the ground. Then the Fox ran up and, before the Eagle's eyes, devoured them every one.

THE OX AND THE FROG

THE OX AND THE FROG.

A N Ox, as he was drinking at the water's edge, crushed a young Frog underfoot. When the mother Frog came to the spot (for she happened to be away at the time) she asked his brothers where he was. "He is dead, mother," they said; "a few minutes ago a great big four-legged thing came up and crushed him dead with his hoof." Thereupon the Frog began to puff herself out and ask whether the animal was as big as that. "Stop, mother, don't put yourself about," they said; "you will burst in two long before you can make yourself the same size as that beast."

"There, my child, have I not as many buttons
as Lady Golderoy now?"

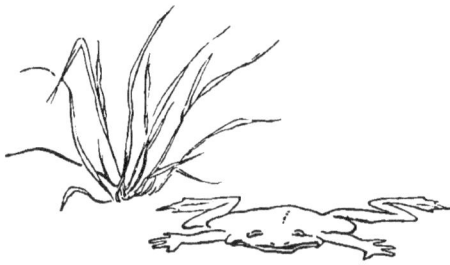

THE HAWK CHASING THE DOVE

THE HAWK CHASING THE DOVE.

A HAWK giving headlong chase to a Dove rushed after it into a farmstead, and was captured by one of the farm men. The Hawk began to coax the man to let him go, saying that he had never done him any harm. "No," rejoined the man; "nor had this Dove harmed you."

www.ingramcontent.com/pod-product-compliance
Lightning Source LLC
Chambersburg PA
CBHW031451270326
41930CB00007B/943